WELLINGTON SQUARE

Which way now?

Characters

 Jamila Patel

Wing Chan

Tessa Potts

Kevin Miller

Mr March

Scenes

Scene 1: By the castle

Mr March is standing beside the bus with Jamila and Wing Chan. He is pointing to a map.

Mr March: Right, this is where you start from. The cross on the map is where you have to get to.

Jamila: How long should it take us?

Mr March: About two hours if you understand the map.

Wing Chan: I understand the map but I've never done anything like this before.

(Mr March climbs into the bus and calls out of the window.)

Mr March: You'll be OK. I'm going to take Tessa and Kevin to where they are starting. See you in two hours.

(Mr March drives off.)

3

Wing Chan: (looking at the map)
OK, let's see where we're going.
Let's see if we understand the
map.

Jamila: I think we have to go through
some trees.

Wing Chan: (pointing away from the castle)
There are some trees over there.
I think they are the trees that are
on the map.

Jamila: Come on then. Let's get started
and get back quickly.

(They set off towards the trees.)

Jamila: Where to now?

Wing Chan: (looking at the map)
It looks like we have to come out of these trees by a canal.

Jamila: We'd better keep going then. It's spooky in here.

(sound of rustling leaves)

Wing Chan: Sh! What's that noise?

Jamila: I don't know.

Wing Chan: It might be a dangerous animal.

Jamila: (smiling)
If we see an elephant we'll know we've gone the wrong way!

Wing Chan: Very funny!

Jamila: Let's sit down on that fallen tree and look at the map.

(They sit and study the map.)

Scene 2: In the countryside

Tessa and Kevin are standing by a gate to a field. Kevin is looking at the map.

Tessa: We can't stay here all day looking at the map. Let's get going.

Kevin: OK. I'm just trying to understand where we have to go.

Tessa: (peering over Kevin's shoulder at the map) I think we should go through this gate and across the field.

7

Kevin: (looking horrified)
No way! That field might have a
dangerous bull in it!

Tessa: (standing on the gate to have a
look)
No. No bull, but I can see an
elephant!

Kevin: (scowling)
Very funny!

Tessa: Come on. We have to get going.
We've only got two hours.

(They trudge across the field.)

(Kevin and Tessa have stopped at the other side of the field.)

Kevin: Where to now?

Tessa: You've got the map. Have a look.

Kevin: I think we're here.
(points to place on the map)
And the cross is there so we have to go through those trees over there.
(points to trees in the distance)

Tessa: OK, come on then.

Kevin: If we go right through the trees, we should come out near a canal.

Tessa: (sounding doubtful) I hope you're right.

Kevin: I'm sure I'm right. I understand the map.

(They go into the trees.)

I want something to eat. Let's stop and have something to eat.

Tessa: Sh! What's that noise?

Kevin: The elephant you saw in the field might have followed us!

Tessa: Very funny! Be quiet. I can hear talking.

Kevin: Wow! A talking elephant!

Tessa: Oh, shut up.

(Voices can now be heard.)

Kevin: That's Wing Chan.

Tessa: And Jamila. Come on.

(They move quickly through the trees to where Jamila and Wing Chan are sitting.)

Jamila: (jumping up)
Oh, it's you. You gave us a fright!

Wing Chan: Do you know where you're going? I think we're lost.

Tessa: Let's stay together and find a way out of these trees.

(They nod in agreement and set off.)

Scene 3: By the canal

The children have come out of the wood by a canal.
They are looking pleased with themselves.

Kevin: Now we've found the canal, can we have something to eat?

Wing Chan: OK, but we can't be too long or we will never make it in two hours.

Jamila: We will have something to eat and look at the map.

(They all sit down at the edge of the canal and unpack their rucksacks.)

13

Tessa: (looking at the map)
It isn't easy to see where we should go next. Do we follow the canal or do we go over there? (points in both directions)

Jamila: (getting up to look at the map with Tessa)
Yes, I see. There's the trees and there's the cross. I think we go over there.

Kevin: Let me have a look.

Wing Chan: Kevin, just finish eating so we can get going again.

Kevin: (getting up and going over to Tessa)
I can understand the map better than Tessa. I'll tell you the way we should go.
(He makes a grab for the map.)

Tessa: (sounding cross)
Leave it, Kevin!

(She moves the map quickly out of Kevin's reach.)

Kevin: (tripping and falling into the canal)
Oh!

(Splash! The children scramble to their feet.)

Tessa: Kevin! Kevin! Are you all right?

Kevin: (spluttering and coughing)
No, I'm not all right! Help me out of here!

Wing Chan: Kevin! Swim back here and we can help you out of the water.

Jamila: The water must be very cold.

(They help Kevin out of the canal, trying not to laugh.)

Kevin: That was a stupid thing to do Tessa.

Tessa: (looking very cross)
I didn't do anything! You tried to get the map!

(Kevin is wringing out his T shirt and picking weeds off himself.)

Wing Chan: Come on you two. We must get going.

Kevin: I'm not walking like this!

Jamila: Then you'll just have to stay here on your own!

(The others pack up their rucksacks and begin to walk off.)

Kevin: (shouting)
I'm not staying here on my own! Wait for me!
(He hurriedly packs his rucksack and 'squelches' after them.)

Scene 4: In the countryside

The children are walking along with Kevin a few steps behind.

Kevin: How much longer do we have to walk?

Tessa: (stopping suddenly)
Wait a minute! I have seen that field before!

Kevin: And that gate! We climbed that gate and walked across that field two hours ago!

Jamila: (sounding worried)
We are just going round and round!

Wing Chan: (pointing to some trees)
Look. I'm sure those are the trees we have already walked through!

Kevin: (looking smug)
We are lost. So much for you understanding the map, Tessa.

Tessa: You couldn't do any better!

Wing Chan: It's no good getting cross. That won't help.

Jamila: What are we going to do? I don't want to have to stay out here all night. It's spooky.

Kevin: And I'm wet. I'll catch a cold.

All: Oh, shut up Kevin!

(Kevin goes and sits down by the side of the road.)

Wing Chan: Let's keep going. I'm sure we are following the map. It can't be far now.

Kevin: For all you know we could be going the wrong way. I'm sitting right here. Mr March will have to come and look for us.

Jamila: I think Kevin is right. We should wait here until Mr March can find us.

(They all sit down.)

Tessa: Do you think Mr March will have started to look for us yet?

Wing Chan: I don't know.

Kevin: I'm really cold and hungry.

All: Oh, shut up Kevin!

Kevin: What's that?

Jamila: (jumping up)
What?

Kevin: That noise!

(The noise of an engine can be heard in the distance. Mr March drives up and jumps out of the mini bus.)

Mr March: Well done! You all made it to the right spot. You are very good at understanding the map.

(The children all look at one another in surprise.)